A GARDEN STYLE BOOK

LITTLE HERB GARDENS

[SIMPLE SECRETS FOR GLORIOUS GARDENS—INDOORS AND OUT]

GEORGEANNE BRENNAN AND MIMI LUEBBERMANN
PHOTOGRAPHY BY FAITH ECHTERMEYER

CHRONICLE BOOKS
SAN FRANCISCO

Text © 1993 by Georgeanne Brennan
and Mimi Luebbermann.
Photographs Copyright © 1993 Faith Echtermeyer.

Library of Congress Cataloging in Publication Data
Brennan, Georgeanne, 1943-
Little herb gardens: simple secrets for glorious
gardens–indoors and out/by Georgeanne Brennan
and Mimi Luebbermann; photography by
Faith Echtermeyer.
p. cm.
"A Garden Style Book."
Includes bibliographical references (p. 93) and index.
ISBN 0-8118-0249-3 (pb)
1. Herb gardening. 2. Herbs.
3. Container gardening. 4. Cookery (Herbs)
I. Luebbermann, Mimi. II. Title.
SB351.H5B6593 1993
635'.7–dc20   92-25637
                             CIP

Printed in Hong Kong

Cover and interior design by
Aufuldish & Warinner

Editing by Carey Charlesworth

Distributed in Canada by Raincoast Books,
112 East Third Ave., Vancouver, B.C. V5T 1C8

10 9 8 7 6 5 4 3

Chronicle Books
275 Fifth Street
San Francisco, CA 94103

Dedicated to:

Daniel and Arann

(MCL)

Charlotte Kimball

(GB)

Introduction

One of the most basic and sensual of all gardening pleasures is growing fresh herbs and using them in preparing our daily food.

Even an act so simple as clipping a few aromatic leaves of Italian parsley from a single windowsill plant and sprinkling them across a salad activates the senses—visual, tactile, olfactory, and above all gustatory.

¶Herbs, by definition, are garden plants that provide flavoring and seasoning for food, and for this use, fresh herbs have no culinary equivalent. The oils in the herbs that create the characteristic flavor are most intense when the herbs are fresh. Dried herbs, which have lost some of their oils, have culinary value, but they are not a substitute for the sharp scent and taste of the earth, water, and sun that fresh herbs bring to food.

¶Herbs can be grown successfully in small spaces, both inside and outside, and that is the subject of this book. Everyone can experience the pleasure of growing and using fresh herbs, even if the only space available is the corner of a table or a windowsill.

¶Herbs have a number of virtues that should encourage even the most apprehensive gardener. They are relatively inexpensive to buy and to grow. Many kinds of herbs can be easily grown from seed, including arugula, basil, dill, and cilantro, which spring up almost immediately after planting. Other herbs, rosemary and lavender for example, are primarily grown from rooted cuttings, which can be purchased in small, inexpensive sizes from garden centers and nurseries.

¶Herbs are relatively pest and disease free, which tends to make them low-maintenance plants. Water, soil, fertilizer, and a little place in the sun are all they need to grow.

¶Hundreds of plants are classified as herbs, especially when used for remedies, but we have included only the most commonly used and easily grown culinary herbs. In some instances the same herb makes two or more appearances: arugula and rosemary, for example. Arugula is as luscious and nutty grown inside in a container as it is grown outside in a small garden space, so it is presented both ways. Rosemary too can be grown inside and outside, potted or not, among other Mediterranean herbs.

¶Throughout the book we offer some ideas about the ways we use herbs in everyday cooking. Thyme and rosemary fill the cavities of our roasting

Contents

POTTED HERBS TO GROW ON A WINDOWSILL OR FIRE ESCAPE   23

POTTED HERBS TO GROW ON AN INSIDE PORCH   35

OUTDOOR POTTED HERBS   47

chickens. Nasturtium leaves and blossoms are part of our salad greens, and tarragon is chopped into salads and tucked around poaching fish. In the final chapter we discuss the basics of making herbed vinegars, oils, sorbets, and biscotti.

¶In writing this book we have laughingly compared notes about our early herb gardens. Both of us were full of trepidation as we dug up patches of ground, carefully smoothing, raking, and watering herb-gardens-to-be. Would the tiny seeds really grow into plants like the ones in the books? Would the transplants live? What would the herbs taste like, if they did survive and grow? (For the most part, we were growing things we had neither tasted nor seen.) Some seeds sprouted and grew quickly, like the basil and the dill, while the parsley seed took several weeks to finally put its first leaves through the ground. By mid-summer, what had been two tiny mint plants had become huge bushes, and the thyme had tripled in size. All the herbs taken from those early gardens imparted the most wonderful flavors to everything we cooked, and the herbs we fell in love with then are still the most prominent ones in our gardens today.

CHARACTERISTICS OF HERBS

Herbs are often grouped as if they all had the same botanical characteristics. In fact, herbs belong to a wide range of genera and species and there is as much botanical difference between bay laurel and basil as there is between lettuce and apples.

¶Herbs are treated as a group based on usage. *Hortus Third*, a standard botanical reference, says that "As defined in a horticultural rather than botanical sense, herbs are those garden plants employed in a secondary way in cooking for flavoring and seasoning, as garnishes for foods, and also as domestic remedies."

¶Herbs may be annuals, perennials, or biennials. Annuals are plants that complete their life cycle within a year. They germinate, grow, bloom, fertilize, produce seed, and die. Basil, arugula, and cilantro are examples of annual herbs.

¶Perennials are plants that live more than two years, and many of them, considerably longer. Perennials include both trees and shrubs, but generally the term perennial is used in reference to herbaceous plants. Some perennials lose their leaves and become dormant, as do oregano and lemon verbena. Others, such as tarragon, die back completely in winter. Still other perennials, including rosemary and lavender, retain their leaves but during winter do not produce new growth.

¶Biennials live only two years and take that long to complete their life cycle, growing the first year and reproducing the second. Parsley is one of the biennial herbs. Short-lived perennials are often grouped with the biennials.

¶Annual herbs are quick to grow and to harvest. They almost unfailingly perform well in full sun in nearly any garden soil or potting mix, providing they have adequate nutrients. Whether or not they reseed themselves depends upon the growing climate and conditions.

¶Perennials are extremely diverse, and generalizations about growing them are difficult to make. Perennial herbs are grown from seed and from vegetative cuttings, although they are slower to grow and to harvest from seed than are annual herbs. Many perennials are grown from vegetative cuttings. Vegetative reproduction is the process of forming independent plants from cuttings that are taken from desirable plants and induced to grow roots. Since all the original tissue of each cutting comes from one parent, it will be genetically identical to that parent.

¶Herb plants, seedlings, and seeds of all kinds are available in nurseries, garden centers, and specialty garden shops and from mail-order catalogues. If you have time and patience, you may want to try growing your own perennial herbs from seed. If, on the other hand, time (or patience) is at a premium, you will probably want to purchase perennials as plants. Most of the annuals are easy to grow from seed, and even the most intimidated novice should give growing annuals from seed a try. To see the first little leaves coming through the surface of the soil is quite thrilling and provides an altogether different sort of satisfaction from that given by nurturing a transplant.

About growing herbs

When we first started growing herbs in kitchen gardens, Mimi in Virginia and Georgeanne in California, neither of us had an iota of factual information about how to proceed. As liberal arts majors we knew about the romance and lore of herbs in literature and history and were well informed about which herbs were found in the gardens of medieval French chateaux and monasteries, and which ones figured in Shakespeare's sonnets. In spite of our ignorance, most of the herbs we planted thrived, and we harvested them and used them in our cooking every day.

Total ignorance is not an ideal way to start herb gardening, however, so the purpose of this section of the book is to provide a few horticultural and botanical fundamentals about water, soils, potting mixes, prepared ground, fertilizers, and frost protection.

Water

Plants use water to transport nutrients. Generally speaking, the water exists as a column extending from the soil through the roots and up the stem, and out to and through the leaves into the atmosphere. All the water molecules have tremendously powerful attractive forces among them, so when one molecule is evaporated from a leaf's surface it pulls the molecule below it up into its previous position, and that molecule does likewise to its successor, and so on like a chain down through the plant.

¶During periods of high evaporation, such as hot or windy days, the rate of water lost from the leaf increases, so more water is pulled in through the roots and up through the plant.

¶Water in the soil can be loose, in the air spaces between soil particles, and also be bound tightly to the surfaces of some soil particles. The loose water is freely available to the plant, but as it is depleted more force is required to remove the other water from the particle surfaces. During times of high evaporation there comes a point where the plant is losing more water than it has the strength to gain, and at that point it wilts.

¶A properly watered plant is one that has constant access to readily available water in the soil, water sufficient to anticipate the hot or windy days' high rates of evaporation. The air in the spaces between the soil particles contains the same gases as our atmosphere, but since most plants cannot carry oxygen from above ground down to the roots and since roots need oxygen to breathe, just as we do, the roots must get their oxygen from the soil atmosphere.

¶When the soil pores are filled with water, oxygen is excluded from them and consequently is not available to the roots. If the soil about the roots is continuously water soaked, plants suffocate because of insufficient oxygen.

¶Water-soaked soil is caused by overwatering or poor drainage or both. Normally, when an area of soil fills with water, gravity pulls the water down through the soil pores, allowing oxygen to fill them in again. Certain factors, such as the lack of a hole in a planting container, prevent this process and cause poor drainage and suffocation.

¶A plant's need for water varies by type, stage of growth, and environmental factors. Some herbs, especially the Mediterranean ones, have adapted to dry climates by evolving mechanisms that permit them to survive drought, either by storing water or by reducing water loss. Others, like mint, have adaptations that allow them to grow well in high-moisture, low-oxygen soils.

The best way to gauge your plant's water needs is to keep these basics in mind while you grow your plant, noticing how it responds.

SOILS, POTTING MIXES, AND PREPARED GROUND

Soil is a mixture of the three soil particles—sand, silt, and clay—plus any organic matter. Sand is chemically inactive, so it is the clay and silt and the organic matter that are involved in the complex exchanges of water and plant nutrients. Sand, however, is by far the largest in size of the particles, so the presence of sand means that there will be correspondingly large spaces between soil particles. These very large soil pores allow good drainage, high oxygen concentrations, and good horizontal water movement.

¶The organic matter in soils is old plant material, decomposing under constant attack by bacteria and fungi. Over time these liberate mineral elements that are essential to other plants for their growth.

¶An ideal soil would be composed of a mixture of sand, silt, clay, and organic matter in proportions that would allow good drainage and aeration yet have adequate water and nutrient-holding capabilities. A good loamy soil is about 60 percent sand, 20 percent silt, and 20 percent clay. Most soils are well under 5 percent organic matter.

¶Commercial potting mixes are much, much higher in organic matter and much, much lower in sand. The addition of sand to these mixes greatly increases the ease of adequately watering them.

¶To prepare garden ground for planting, first remove existing plant material such as weeds or plants that you no longer want in the garden ground. With a shovel, a spade, or a machine, such as a rototiller, turn the soil over to a depth of 12 to 18 inches. Water the turned soil and allow any undesirable seeds that may be in the ground to sprout. When the ground is dry enough to work, remove the plant material once again. Using a hoe or shovel, break the soil up into small particles. Rake the surface smooth. The ground is now prepared for planting.

FERTILIZERS

The major nutrients needed for plant growth are nitrogen, phosphorus, and potassium. A plant removes these nutrients from the soil and uses them as it grows, so fertilizer is used to replace them, allowing continued growth. Nutrient needs are greatest during periods of rapid growth, typically spring and summer.

¶Generally commercial fertilizers list their content as the percentage of each nutrient, in the order nitrogen-phosphorus-potassium, so a 20-10-10 fertilizer would be 20 percent nitrogen, 10 percent each phosphorus and potassium.

¶Nitrogen is the most consumed nutrient, used heavily in the green vegetative growth. A yellowing of leaves, particularly older leaves, often indicates a deficiency of nitrogen and that it is time to add fertilizer. Phosphorus and potassium are necessary for a wide range of plant functions especially during periods of rapid growth.

¶Fertilizers come in many different forms, both dry and liquid. We recommend using organic fertilizers, which are increasingly available, and we find for most herbs, especially container-planted herbs, that an all-purpose or fish emulsion liquid fertilizer adequately supplies nutrient needs.

FROST PROTECTION

Cold temperatures can freeze the water inside plants, causing it to expand and rupture the plant's walls. Fleshy plants with soft walls, like nasturtiums, are in more danger in cold weather than plants with thick or woody stems, like rosemary.

¶Susceptible plants should be protected from frosts and freezes. Depending on your plants and the harshness of your climate, there is an array of ways to mitigate the effects.

¶During a frost it is often necessary only to cover a plant to protect its leaves from contact with the briefly freezing air, but a hard frost can be a different matter. The first line of defense is to cover the plants by wrapping or mulching them, or to provide a heat source to warm the air around them to above freezing. The one sure way to prevent damage is to move the plants inside.

POTTED
HERBS TO
GROW ON A
WINDOWSILL
OR FIRE
ESCAPE

In a space as small as a windowsill, the edge of a fire escape, or a balcony corner, an herb garden can thrive. Perfect for people in an urban apartment where every bit of space is at a premium, the undemanding herb gardens in this section require only a small container, which can be tucked wherever there is any available space, plus four to six hours of sunlight a day. ❧ Some of the herbs, such as arugula and cilantro, grow quickly from seed and can be reseeded every few weeks for an ongoing supply. Others, such as parsley, are easily raised from transplanted seedlings. Garlic and onion greens grow from bulbs that supply most of their nourishment, and they send up delectable green shoots only a few weeks after being planted. ❧ An elegant member of the geranium family, the scented geranium, thrives happily indoors, and only a leaf or two will scent a creamy pudding. You can steep the leaves to brew a tea. ❧ The simplest windowsill garden of all, though, is not even planted. Fragrant bunches of store-bought fresh herbs can be maintained on kitchen windowsills or counters for days.

Quick-growing Arugula, Cilantro, or Dill from Seed

The almost-instant gratification received from growing arugula, cilantro, or dill is reason enough to plant them. Each sprouts and grows quickly. Arugula leaves pop though the soil in three or four days. Success appears before your eyes. Cilantro emerges shortly thereafter, in five or six days, while feathery dill tips come through the soil in about ten days. Any of the three can be put to use within a few weeks, to flavor salads, soups, and sauces and to sprinkle on pizzas and sandwiches. ¶ Grow any or all of these herbs in small, window-sized pots, and replant with fresh seeds after a couple of months. A steady supply of succulent, tender leaves is your reward. Spring and fall produce especially good harvests. All three herbs quickly send up central stalks, flower, and go to seed during summer, and in winter germination is slower. ¶ Arugula is also called rocket, garden rocket, and roquette. Cilantro is also known as Chinese parsley and coriander.

¶ **HOW TO DO IT** ¶ Make sure your container has a drainage hole in the bottom. Cover the hole with a little gravel, a few small rocks, or bits of broken pottery. ¶ Fill the container with potting mix to within 1/2 inch of the rim. Soak the potting mix with water until it is thoroughly moist. Scoop out approximately 1/2 cup of the moist mix and set aside. Space seeds about 1/2 inch apart and press them into the mix gently with the palm of your hand. ¶ Sprinkle the seeds with the reserved mix, providing a 1/4-inch soil cover. Pat the potting mix covering down. ¶ Keep the potting mix moist and fertilize every two weeks with a liquid fertilizer.

Arugula, Cilantro, or Dill
Eruca vesicaria sativa; Coriandrum sativum; Anethum graveolens

❧

What You Need
1 packet seed
Container at least 4 inches deep and 8 inches in diameter
Gravel, small rocks, or bits of broken pottery
Potting mix
Liquid fertilizer

❧

Growing Conditions
At least a half-day of direct sun

❧

When to Buy
Arugula and cilantro seeds: year-round from mail-order catalogues
Dill seeds: spring and summer from garden centers or nurseries as well as mail-order catalogues

❧

When to Plant
Year-round, but spring and fall are most favorable

❧

When to Harvest
Pick young leaves in approximately 25 to 35 days

❧

ITALIAN PARSLEY

*I*f you have only room to grow a single potted herb, Italian flat-leaf parsley is a good choice. Its dark jade-green leaves are richly pungent and only a few are needed to flavor omelettes, salads, soups, and stews. Kept healthy, the plant will quickly grow new leaves to replace the ones you use. ¶ Parsley seeds are rather slow and uneven in their germination, so for quicker and more reliable results you might buy seedlings of Italian flat parsley. Look for them in 2-inch pots or six-packs. Three plants will have ample room to grow for several months when transplanted to a 6-inch container. ¶ When spring days lengthen, parsley plants tend to send up woody seed stalks, then flower and go to seed. Break off these stalks to encourage leafy growth a bit longer. ¶ **HOW TO DO IT** ¶ First, make sure your container has a drainage hole in the bottom. Cover the hole with a little gravel, a few small rocks, or bits of broken pottery. ¶ Fill a sink, bowl, or bucket with water, then submerge your seedlings, still in their pots or trays. Let them stand until air bubbles cease to appear. ¶ While the seedlings are soaking, fill the container with potting mix to within 1/2 inch of the rim. Soak the potting mix with water until it is thoroughly moist. ¶ Scoop out a hole for each of your transplants deep enough that the roots will extend straight down, and not bend. Put the transplants in the holes, filling in any empty spaces with the reserved soil. Pat down the surface, then water to fill in any air pockets. ¶ Fertilize every two to three weeks with a liquid fertilizer and keep the soil thoroughly moist.

Italian Parsley

Petroselinum crispum var. neopolitanum

❧

What You Need

3 or 4 parsley plants
Container at least 6 inches in diameter
and 6 inches or more deep
Gravel, small rocks, or bits
of broken pottery
Potting mix
Liquid fertilizer

❧

Growing Conditions

At least one-third day direct sun

❧

When to Buy

Year-round at nurseries and
garden centers

❧

When to Plant

Year-round

❧

When to Harvest

Start picking leaves when plants have
2 inches of new growth

❧

Rose-scented Geranium

*G*ently rub the leaves of a rose-scented geranium plant and a sensual rose fragrance immediately fills the air and clings to your fingertips. Close your eyes and you are transported, standing in a rose garden in full summer bloom. ¶ Completely unrelated to the rose, this geranium gets it scent from volatile oils in the leaves rather than from the small and somewhat insignificant flowers that appear periodically. The slightest pressure upon the leaves will release the scent. Crushed leaves may be steeped in warm water or cream. The liquid will be infused with the rose scent and will flavor icings, custards, or creams. ¶ Rose-scented geranium plants, along with other scented geraniums, can be purchased in many sizes from nurseries. Since these plants are quite quick to increase in size, we suggest starting with a small one, perhaps 4-inch pot size. ¶ A rose-scented geranium will thrive inside on your windowsill or outside on a fire escape or porch, but it will need to overwinter inside in areas where temperatures drop to freezing. ¶ **HOW TO DO IT** ¶ Choose a container at least 6 inches in diameter and 6 inches deep. Make sure your container has a drainage hole in the bottom. Cover the hole with a little gravel, a few small rocks, or bits of broken pottery. ¶ Fill a sink, pan, or bucket with water. Submerge your rose-scented geranium, still in its purchased pot, in the water and let it stand until air bubbles cease to appear. While the plant is soaking, fill the planting container with potting mix to within 1/2 inch of the rim. Soak the potting mix with water until it is thoroughly moist. Remove the geranium from its

Rose-Scented Geranium

Pelargonium graveolens

What You Need

1 plant, 4-inch pot size

Container at least 6 inches in diameter and 6 inches deep

Gravel, small rocks, or bits of broken pottery

Potting mix

Geranium fertilizer or all-purpose liquid fertilizer

Growing Conditions

A half-day or more of direct sun

When to Buy

Year-round from nurseries and specialty mail-order catalogues

When to Plant

Year-round

When to Harvest

Pick leaves to use when the plant shows at least 2 inches of new growth

container and gently shake off the potting mix around its roots. ¶ Scoop out a hole for your rose-scented geranium deep enough for the main root to extend straight down. Put your plant in the hole, gently fanning out the thin side roots, then fill in any empty spaces around the roots with the reserved soil. Pat down the surface and water to fill in any air pockets remaining in the soil. ¶ Whenever the potting mix becomes dry, water your geranium by submerging the entire container in water and letting it stand for at least half an hour or until the potting mix is saturated. ¶ Fertilize every three weeks with a geranium fertilizer mix or with an all-purpose liquid fertilizer. If your plant is kept outside, be sure to bring it inside or otherwise protect it during the winter if frosts or freezes threaten.

Green onions or green garlic

Pack a container with soil and several whole garlic bulbs or a dozen tiny onion sets, and water it. Within a few weeks dozens of bright green leaves will have pushed through the soil. Not only are they cheerful to look at, especially on grim, grey winter days, but the clipped stalks are one of the most flavorsome fresh herbs to have handy for cooking. ¶ For a special occasion, put your growing green onions or green garlic on the table and let your guests do their own snipping. Fresh sprinkles of the greens are the classic toppings for baked potatoes and for Vichyssoise soup, but they can be added to anything from tomato salad to gratinéed potatoes. ¶ Potted onions and garlic are almost foolproof to grow and make wonderful gifts. The potted garlic especially makes an unusual gift for someone who likes to experiment in the kitchen. ¶ **HOW TO DO IT** ¶ For a head of garlic or a half-dozen onion sets, an 8-inch container is ideal. Make sure your container has a drainage hole in the bottom. Cover the hole with a little gravel, a few small rocks, or bits of broken pottery. ¶ Fill the container about half-full with potting mix for the garlic, three-quarters full for onion sets, and soak the mix with water until it is thoroughly moist. Put the whole garlic heads on top of the moist mix, flat side down. Place the onion sets root side down. Cover the garlic or onion sets with moist potting mix to within 1/2 inch of the rim. ¶ Water occasionally, keeping the soil lightly moist but not soggy.

Garlic or Onions
Allium sativum, Allium cepa

What You Need
2 or 3 whole heads seed garlic or 10 to 12 sets seed onions (see note)
Container at least 8 inches in diameter and 8 to 10 inches deep
Gravel, small rocks, or bits of broken pottery
Potting mix

Growing Conditions
At least one-quarter day of direct sun

When to Buy
Late summer through early spring from garden centers, nurseries, and mail-order catalogues

When to Plant
Fall through spring

When to Harvest
Start clipping green sprouts after several inches of green shoots have appeared, about 3 weeks after planting.

Note: Sometimes garlic heads and small onions purchased at the vegetable market will sprout and grow. Other times they have been treated with a sprouting retardant.

A CUT GARDEN

The simplest herb garden of all is temporary and ephemeral, yet it supplies its owner with daily fresh herbs for cooking and fills the kitchen with the scent of far-away places. Soft, pale grey sage leaves bring the smell of high, arid plateaus, and shrubby stems of thyme recall the dry hillsides of Southern France or Tuscany. Parsley, tarragon, basil, and dill bring the comforting smell of the damp earth on the edges of meadows and along stream sides. ¶ No matter what herbs you choose for your cut garden, select only fresh, healthy-looking ones. Do not buy any that have dark spots or signs of yellowing or that are limp. No amount of loving care can reverse decay. ¶ Herbs with woody stems such as sage, thyme, rosemary, oregano, and marjoram are the longest lasting, with tarragon and basil next. Dill and mint are brief, lasting just a few days before beginning to yellow, but are among the most aromatic. ¶ **HOW TO DO IT** ¶ Purchase these herbs precut in the produce department of a supermarket, each bunch most likely bound with a shiny wire twist tie. Take off the tie, and put each bunch of herbs in its own glass, lining up the glasses on your windowsill to make a pleasing arrangement. ¶ Enjoy and use the herbs as long as you can, and don't bemoan their demise at the end of a week or so. Change the water daily. Discard any decaying leaves.

A Cut Garden

❧

What You Need
Bunches of any of your favorite herbs
Glasses of water

❧

Growing Conditions
Indirect sunlight

¶

When to Buy
Year-round at supermarkets and greengrocers, and during summer and fall at farmers' markets

❧

When to Harvest
Start using the herbs right away

❧

POTTED
HERBS TO
GROW ON
AN INSIDE
PORCH

Inside porches differ from outside porches in several important ways for the purposes of plants. An inside porch is enclosed, generally by glass windows. The windows allow light and can be opened to allow fresh air to circulate. Unlike an outside porch, an inside porch provides protection from the elements. Because of this, an inside porch is a good place to grow tender potted herbs during winter. Calendulas, basils, and nasturtiums that would perish outside thrive on an inside porch. ❧ The inside porch also offers shelter for elegant specimen potted plants, such as dwarf kumquat trees or scented geraniums. They can use its protection in winter, or the inside porch may be their permanent home. For potted herbs that are too large to perch on a windowsill, as well, the porch offers an alternate home. ❧ In the past, glassed-in porches were de rigueur in many homes, where they were built specifically for the purpose of housing indoor plant collections. Proud owners of exotic plants displayed and tended their treasures in the glass rooms that captured the light, sun, and warmth necessary for growth. Among the special plants grown were elegant clipped topiaries of bay laurel and blue-flowering rosemary, three and four feet high and in prominent places. Brilliant mahogany and crimson nasturtiums cascaded from embossed pots sitting atop decorative pillars. Huge baskets planted with orange and yellow calendulas were stair-stepped on hand-forged metal etagères of the period. Deep purple basil plants were tucked among equally colorful ornamentals, encouraged to send up their flowering spikes of lavender flowers. ❧ As lovely as a glassed-in porch is, any room will serve for growing your plants that has one-half to three-quarters of a day of sunlight. It further requires only space enough for you to devote to a large potted herb or two.

Cascading nasturtiums

Nasturtiums, now considered rather old fashioned and unsophisticated, were once so popular that seed companies vied with one another to breed astonishing new varieties. Their multitude of colors captured the attention of the amateur-gardening public. The plants are easy to grow and quick to develop beautiful blossoms, in colors from cream to scarlet and all shades of gold, orange, and red. Nasturtiums also have aesthetically pleasing twisting, vining stems, and leaves so thin and clear that the light passes through them. ¶ A large planter of cascading nasturtiums makes a dramatic accent for any room, and the sweet, honey scent they exude is pleasing as well. In addition, the leaves and blossoms are deliciously edible, and like watercress, a relative of nasturtium, have a peppery taste that makes them a good salad ingredient. ¶ Many of the newer varieties of nasturtium are not vining or trailing types but bush types, and these will not form a cascade. ¶ **HOW TO DO IT** ¶ Soak the nasturtium seeds overnight. This allows the seed to fill itself with water and to start the growth process before it is planted. ¶ Choose a large container, about 24 inches long and 12 inches or more deep. Make sure your container has a drainage hole in the bottom. Cover the hole with a little gravel, a few small rocks, or bits of broken pottery. ¶ Fill the container with potting mix to within 1/2 inch of the rim. Soak the potting mix with water until it is thoroughly moist. Scoop out 2 cups of the moist soil from the surface and set aside. Plant the soaked nasturtium seeds 3 inches apart and sprinkle the seeds with the reserved soil, providing 1/2 inch of soil cover. Pat the soil covering down. ¶ Nasturtiums need to be kept moist. The leaves have a large surface area, and moisture evaporates from them at a high rate. Spray the leaves with a mister and water the plants frequently. Fertilize every two to three weeks with a liquid fertilizer. Remove dead leaves and blossoms.

Nasturtium, Vining Type

Tropaeolum majus

❧

What You Need

50 nasturtium seeds, or about 1/4 ounce
Container at least 24 inches long
or in diameter, and at least 12 inches deep
Gravel, small rocks, or bits
of broken pottery
Potting mix

❧

Growing Conditions

At least a half-day direct sun

❧

When to Buy

Seed is available in spring from mail-order catalogues and in spring and summer
at garden centers and nurseries

❧

When to Plant

Year-round

❧

When to Harvest

Use blossoms in approximately 75 days,
but young leaves can be used sooner

❧

POTTED BAY LAUREL

A fresh bay laurel leaf bears no resemblance to the dried leaf. The fresh leaf, slick, shiny, and a vibrant, dark forest green, exudes a clean, sharp scent when rubbed between your fingers. In spring, when the new leaves appear, they are a bright, chartreuse green, turning darker as they mature. ¶ One leaf, perhaps two, is enough to flavor a whole pot roast or a large, simmering kettle of homemade minestrone. Yellow onions flavored with a few bay leaves and cooked down to a thick, golden confit make a fine sandwich spread or pizza topping. ¶ When grown in the most favorable circumstances, the Laurus nobilis tree soars to over 50 feet high, but it is also very successful in a container. It can easily be grown inside as a bushy shrub, or for the patient and very romantic, as a precisely pruned and elegant topiary. **¶ HOW TO DO IT ¶** Buy a one- or two-year-old bay laurel, also called sweet bay or Grecian bay. The younger one will probably be in a 1-gallon can and the two-year-old in a 5-gallon can. The younger one will be smaller, of course, but there is less chance that it will be rootbound. ¶ Choose a container at least 18 inches in diameter and 24 inches deep. Make sure your container has a drainage hole in the bottom. Cover the hole with a little gravel, a few small rocks, or bits of broken pottery. Proper drainage is especially important for bay laurels since the roots are prone to rotting if they stand in soggy soil too long. ¶ Fill your container about half-full of potting mix and soak it until it is thoroughly moist. Fill the sink, bucket, or a large bowl with water and submerge the plant, still in its container. Let it stand until air bubbles cease to appear. Remove it from its container and examine the roots. ¶ If the roots ✒

go around and around the sides in the shape of the container, cut them back to the beginning of the circular growth. Now trim the top growth a like amount, so the plant system is in balance with the revised root system. For example, if you have trimmed away 2 inches of root growth, you should trim an equal amount of top growth. ¶ Hold your plant upright in the container and fill around the roots with moist potting mix, packing well as you go. Water to fill in any air pockets. ¶ If you have room, put the potted tree outside during the warm summer months. Water when the potting mix has dried out. To observe this, run a knife down the side of the planted container and bring up a sample. Fertilize once a month from March through November with a liquid fertilizer high in nitrogen, phosphorus, and potash.

PURPLE BASIL BUSH

Deliciously edible, purple basil is also a beautiful ornamental plant. The leaves are a deep, royal purple and are sometimes flecked with green. The stems are also deep purple. The plants easily grow to 2 feet or more, sending up early flowering spikes composed of dozens of tiny lavender flowers. When crushed or even brushed against, the leaves release a fragrant, clovelike scent. ¶ If you keep cutting back the flowering stalks, the plant will become increasingly large and bushy. The flowers are quite edible and have the same flavor as the leaves, but slightly milder, with a paperlike texture. The leaves and flowers are both wonderful sprinkled across sliced tomatoes.

¶ **HOW TO DO IT** ¶ Potted purple basil may be started from seeds or from seedlings. Make sure your container has a drainage hole in the bottom. Cover the hole with a little gravel, a few small rocks, or bits of broken pottery. ¶ Choose a container at least 8 inches across and 10 inches deep. Basil plants put down deep roots. Plan on one container for each mature plant. ¶ Fill the container with potting mix to within 1/2 inch of the rim. Soak the potting mix with water until it is thoroughly moist. Scoop out approximately 1 cup of the moist soil from the top and set this aside, if you are using seeds. For a transplant, scoop out a hole about 6 inches deep. ¶ If you are using seeds, space them about 2 inches apart and cover them with the reserved soil, providing 1/4 inch of soil cover. Pat the soil cover down. Eventually, thin the seedlings that grow until only a single ➹

plant remains. ¶ If you are transplanting purchased seedlings, first submerge each, still in its container, in a sink, bowl, or bucketful of water and let it stand until air bubbles cease to appear. Gently remove it and its potting mix from the container and put it in the hole you prepared. Fill in any empty spaces around the roots with the soil you scooped out. Pat down the surface. Water to fill in any air pockets. ¶ Fertilize every two to three weeks with a liquid fertilizer. Cut back flowering stalks if you wish to encourage leafy, bushy growth. Keep basil plants away from cold drafts.

CALENDULAS

For masses of instant hot color inside, calendula is the perfect choice. Fluorescent orange and gold daisylike flowers blanket the relatively small plant, which blooms repeatedly. For centuries, calendula was considered one of the most important of the herbs for cooking, dyes, and magical uses, but during the twentieth century its culinary qualities have been overlooked in favor of its purely floral attributes. ¶ In the past, one of the important culinary uses for calendula was as a substitute for the rare and very expensive saffron. Calendula petals were dried, and then ground into a fine powder. Calendula powder gives rice and sauces, for example, the same intense yellow coloring that true saffron threads impart. ¶ For a simple, one-step use, add calendula petals to salads and pasta dishes of all kinds. As with all edible flowers, be absolutely certain that they have not been sprayed or otherwise treated with a harmful or even potentially harmful chemical. ¶ **HOW TO DO IT** ¶ Although calendula is easily grown from seed, the seedlings are readily available almost anywhere plants are sold. Because the seedlings are sold with buds ready to burst into bloom, we think they are a better choice than seeds if you want bright, cheerful color quickly. ¶ For five calendula plants, choose a container at least 24 inches across and 12 inches deep. Your plants will grow to a foot or more in height. Make sure your container has a drainage hole in the bottom. Cover the hole with a little gravel, a few small rocks, or bits of broken pottery. ¶ Fill a sink, bowl, or bucket with water. Submerge your seedlings, still in their pots or trays, and let them stand until air bubbles cease to appear. ¶ While the seedlings are soaking, fill the container to which you are going to transplant them

Calendula

Calendula officinalis

What You Need

5 seedlings, 2-inch or
4-inch pot size
Container at least 24 inches in diameter
and 12 inches deep
Gravel, small rocks, or bits
of broken pottery
Potting mix
Liquid fertilizer

Growing Conditions

At least a half-day of direct sun

When to Buy

Late winter through early summer
from garden centers and nurseries; also
in fall in mild winter areas

When to Plant

As soon as seedlings are available
in your area

When to Harvest

Use the flowers as soon as the plant
has bloomed

with potting mix to within 1/2 inch of the rim. Soak the mix with water until it is thoroughly moist. Scoop out holes 4 inches apart and approximately 6 inches deep. Gently remove the transplants and their surrounding potting mix from the containers and put them in the prepared holes. Fill in around their roots with potting mix and pat down the surface. Water to fill in any air pockets. ¶ As you water your calendula do not sprinkle water on the leaves, as this may invite fungal diseases, to which calendulas are susceptible. Instead, water at the roots. Keep soil moist but not soggy. Fertilize every three weeks with a liquid fertilizer. As blooms die, remove them to ensure new growth.

A ROSEMARY TOPIARY STANDARD

If you have patience and vision, growing a rosemary topiary standard will provide you with many hours of pleasure. Topiaries are plants that have been trained, primarily by staking and pruning, to grow treelike on a single, thickened stem, which becomes the "trunk." The branching, leafy portion of the plant is pruned and clipped into a specific shape, ranging from the formally geometric to fanciful, mythical animals. ¶ Rosemary has a particularly woody stem and lends itself quite easily to the will and skill of the patient gardener. A rosemary topiary standard—a trunk topped with a round ball—must be grown from a plant that starts with a straight stem. One way to start is with a small, healthily growing 6- to 8-inch tall upright, not prostrate, rosemary plant that has a straight central stem. By clipping and pruning you will train it to the shape you desire. ¶ If you really want a topiary but are uncertain whether you have the time and patience to start one from the very beginning, purchase one of the small, already trained specimens in one of several different shapes. They are readily available through better nurseries, garden specialty stores, and a few mail-order catalogues. ¶ **HOW TO DO IT** ¶ Submerge the rosemary plant, still in its purchased container, in a sink or bucket of water until air bubbles cease to appear. ¶ Choose a container about 6 inches in diameter and 8 to 10 inches deep for a 4-inch pot size rosemary plant, or a correspondingly larger container for a larger size plant. Make sure the container has a hole for drainage. Cover the hole with gravel, a few rocks, or bits of broken pottery. Rosemary needs particularly good drainage. Cover with about 3 inches of moist potting mix. ¶ Gently remove the rosemary plant from its pot, its potting mix intact, and put the plant into its new container. Gently but firmly pack moist potting mix around the roots, filling the container. Pat the surface smooth and then water to fill in any air pockets. ¶ With your fingers or with pruning clippers, remove all the ✐

Note: When you take leaves for cooking, keep in mind the eventual form for which you are striving. It may take up to 12 months for the realization of the topiary form.

leaves and any side shoots from the lower two-thirds of the plant. Put a thin, straight bamboo stick alongside the rosemary plant down to the bottom of the pot. Tie the rosemary plant to the stick with raffia or garden tape, being careful not to tie so tightly as to cut into the growing stem. ¶ Once the topiary is as tall as you want—12 to 14 inches in a 6-inch container, for example—clip off the new leafy growth at the top. Side branches will begin to develop, and the round ball you are visualizing will begin to fill out. As it does, you can clip wayward pieces that stray outside the shape you are creating. ¶ Fertilize your growing rosemary every two or three weeks with a liquid fertilizer. Remove leaves that sprout from the stem. Repot if the roots begin to creep out the drainage hole, a sign that the plant has outgrown its container.

OUTDOOR

POTTED

HERBS

There are several reasons to consider growing selected herbs in outdoor pots even when you have garden ground available. Pots or enclosed raised beds are especially suitable to contain herbs that spread, such as mint and sorrel. Container planting also dramatizes singularly attractive specimen plants, like Spanish lavender with its twisting foliage and spiked purple flowers, or lemon verbena, noteworthy for its graceful arching branches as well as its seductive scent. Herbs with similar growing requirements can be planted together in the same pot or planted in several pots and kept in the same location to create planting themes. Also, obviously, herbs that can't survive the winter in the ground can be planted in pots that can be moved in and out of the weather. ❧ Plants of unusual basil varieties grouped together make a subtle study in variations of leaf shape, color, size, and scent, yet all are recognizable as basil. In a slightly more complex planting, the herbs that grow wild in the Mediterranean basin are grown together in the same container—rosemary, thyme, oregano, and sage. Here the growth habits, leaf shapes and sizes, scents, and colors of the different herbs vary tremendously, but all combine to make a harmonious whole reminiscent of the herbs' native habitats. ❧ For the specimen and theme plantings, beautiful and intriguing containers are called for. To our thinking, few containers compete with the large, classic terra-cotta garden jars. Manufactured in natural finishes and in various traditional Mediterranean glazes, these jars are available at most specialty nurseries or garden shops. ❧ Having potted herbs outside in addition to your garden plantings enriches the landscape and offers you the opportunity to grow herbs that are too invasive for the garden or too delicate to survive outside during the winter.

Exotic basils

A single container filled with several basils, perhaps lettuce leaf, cinnamon, lemon, Thai, and purple, offers a wide choice of seasonings throughout summer and well into fall. Although each basil has a distinctive appearance and taste, they all have the same water, soil, and sun requirements, so they can be grown together successfully in a single container. ¶ The curling, slightly quilted leaves of light green lettuce-leaf basil are the size of a child's hand. Its flavor is similar to that of Italian large-leaf basil but milder, making it a good choice for salads, pestos, and other traditional basil uses. ¶ Cinnamon basil has small, dark green, sharply pointed leaves that are faintly purple on the underside. Its spicy cinnamon flavor mingled with an underlying green basil taste makes it a good choice to flavor game birds and winter squashes. ¶ Tiny, slightly pointed lemon basil leaves are bright green and have the citrus tang we expect from lemon-flavored herbs. Chicken and fish especially are enhanced by lemon basil. ¶ Thai basil resembles cinnamon basil in coloration, but the leaves are larger and more round and the stems are purple, striated with green. Thai basil's exotic scent and taste, as if ordinary basil had been distilled and turned into perfume, are the most dramatic elements of this plant. If you want to use the leaves traditionally, Thai style, chop them into grilled beef salads and peppery sweet and sour soup. ¶ Purple basil—there are several varieties, including 'Dark Opal' and 'Purple Ruffles'—has the most dramatic appearance of all the basils. The leaves often have serrated or ruffled edges, and they and the stems are deep maroon. The eventual seed stalks have tiny lavender flowers. Purple basil's flavor is similar to large-leaf Italian basil, but more pungent. ¶ Grouped together, the soft blending of green and purple hues makes a very attractive container planting that provides a constant mix of scents. ¶ **HOW TO DO IT** ¶ Buy basil seedlings of several different varieties or start your own from seed. For five to six plants, choose a container about 18 inches in diameter and at least 12 inches deep. Make sure your container has a drainage hole ✒

Basil: Cinnamon, Lemon, Thai, Purple, Lettuce Leaf
Ocimum basilicum

❧

What You Need
5 or 6 basil seedlings, chosen from varieties listed above; Container 18 inches in diameter and at least 12 inches deep Gravel, small rocks, or bits of broken pottery Potting mix; Liquid fertilizer

❧

Growing Conditions
Three-quarters to a full day of direct sun

❧

When to Buy
In winter and spring from specialty mail-order catalogues; in spring and early summer from nurseries and specialty garden shops

❧

When to Plant
Late spring or early summer when ground has warmed

❧

When to Harvest
Use the first thinnings, about 30 days after seedlings emerge, or if using transplants, wait until there is several inches of new growth; harvest mature leaves in about 75 days

❧

in the bottom. Cover the hole with a little gravel, a few small rocks, or bits of broken pottery. ¶ Fill a sink, bowl, or bucket with water and submerge your seedlings, still in their pots or trays. Leave them until no more air bubbles appear so that the potting mix is saturated. ¶ While the seedlings are soaking, fill the planting container with potting mix to within 1/2 inch of the rim. Soak the mix with water until it is thoroughly moist. Scoop out holes 4 inches apart for your seedlings. Put the seedlings and their root balls into the holes, packing the potting mix around them. Pat down the surface. Water to fill in any air pockets. ¶ Keep the soil moist but not soggy. If not well watered, basil will become overly pungent and bitter. Fertilize every three weeks with liquid fertilizer. Cut back flowering stalks in order to continue leaf growth.

LEMON VERBENA

The graceful, arching branches, long and delicate pointed leaves, and a sweet, clean lemon fragrance make lemon verbena a choice specimen plant to show off in a container planting. ¶ As with most scented plants, you can release the aroma by simply brushing against the leaves. Gently rubbing the leaves between your fingertips will make the scent intense. ¶ Culinarily, lemon verbena is one of the herbs that serves equally well in both sweet and savory dishes. Only a few gently crushed leaves infuse a cup of whipping cream with a light, pure lemon taste. For savory uses, add the leaves to roasting chickens, poaching fish, and sauces. ¶ **HOW TO DO IT** ¶ Lemon verbena plants are readily available in 1-gallon cans for repotting. The roots need plenty of room, so we suggest a container at least 24 inches in diameter and 24 inches deep to start. Consider repotting again in a year or two as the plant grows and spreads. ¶ Make sure your container has a drainage hole in the bottom. Cover the hole with a little gravel, a few small rocks, or bits of broken pottery. ¶ Fill your container about half-full of potting mix and soak the mix until it is thoroughly moist. Fill a sink, bucket, or large bowl with water and submerge the plant, still in its pot. Let it stand until no more air bubbles emerge. Remove the plant from its pot and examine the roots. If they go around and around at the sides in the shape of the pot, cut them back to the beginning of the circular growth. Trim the top growth a like amount so that the plant system is in balance with the revised root system. For example, if you clip back one-third of the roots, clip back also one-third of the plant's top growth. ¶ Hold your plant upright in the half-full container and fill around the roots with moist potting mix,

Lemon Verbena
Aloysia triphylla, also called
Lippia citriodora

❧

What You Need
1 lemon verbena plant, 1-gallon can size
Container at least 24 inches in diameter
and 24 inches deep
Gravel, small rocks, or bits
of broken pottery
Potting mix
Small pruning clippers
Liquid fertilizer

❧

Growing Conditions
At least a half-day of direct sun

❧

When to Buy
Spring through summer from nurseries
or garden centers

❧

When to Plant
Spring through early summer

❧

When to Harvest
Begin taking leaves to use when the plant
has 2 to 3 inches of new growth

❧

packing well as you go. Fill to within a 1/2 inch of the rim. Pat down the surface, and water to fill in any air pockets. ¶ Water the lemon verbena often enough to keep moisture in the root zone of the plant. The soil mix should not be soggy. Fertilize every three to four weeks. Repot into a larger container when the plant becomes twice its original size, about 2 feet tall. Repot again when it reaches 3 feet tall. After that, it can be kept cut back to 3 feet. In temperate climates, lemon verbena may be left outside year-round, but in other climates it should overwinter inside. If left outside, lemon verbena will lose its leaves in the fall.

FRENCH LAVENDER

French lavender, sometimes mistakenly called Spanish lavender, has grey-green somewhat toothed leaves and soft, deep-purple blossoms. Because its growth habit, unlike the bristling upright English lavender, is open and spreading, it looks relaxed and natural when it is potted. ¶ A Mediterranean terra-cotta jar is an especially good container choice. The lavender's purple flowers are particularly striking spilling against the rose-ocher tones of the terra-cotta, but a wine barrel cut in half or any container of similar size will suit as well. ¶ Although lavender blossoms of all kinds are well known for their use dried in potpourris and sachets, they also have a variety of culinary uses. Lavender ice cream, made with a vanilla custard base, has the delicate underlying scent of lavender blossoms. Finely chopped blossoms combine with almonds to make Provencal-flavored biscotti, and the fresh blossoms also can add an exotic perfume to iced fruit drinks and cream-topped after-dinner drinks. ¶ **HOW TO DO IT** ¶ Purchase a young French lavender plant in a 1- or 2-gallon pot. Choose a container at least 12 inches in diameter and 24 to 36 inches deep with a drainage hole in the bottom. Put a 10-inch layer of gravel or other rocks on the bottom to serve as a drainage layer. Fill the container to within 2 inches of the top with a mixture of potting mix and sand, and soak the mixture until it is thoroughly moist. Scoop out a hole large enough for the roots of the lavender plant. ¶ Submerge the lavender plant, still in its original pot, in a sink or bucket of water until air bubbles cease to appear so that the soil is thoroughly saturated. ¶ Gently remove the plant from its pot and examine its roots. If the roots curl around in the shape of ✐

French Lavender

Lavendula dentata

❧

What You Need

1 plant, 1- to 2-gallon pot size
Container 24 to 36 inches deep, with a
mouth at least 12 inches in diameter
Gravel or small rocks
Potting mix and sand
Small pruning clippers
Liquid or other fertilizer

❧

Growing Conditions

Three-quarters to a full day of direct sun

❧

When to Buy

When plants are still dormant or show new growth but have not yet bloomed

❧

When to Plant

Early spring through summer before bloom occurs

❧

When to Harvest

Start taking sprigs as soon as blooms appear

❧

the pot, cut them back to the beginning of the circular growth. Trim the top growth a like amount so that the plant system is in balance with the revised root system. For example, if you clip back one-third of the roots, clip back also one-third of the top growth. ¶ Put the lavender plant in the prepared container and fill around the roots with the potting mix, patting down the surface. Water again to fill in any air pockets. ¶ Fertilize your lavender plant in spring and cut off old stems in the fall. Water as needed, but do not allow the soil mix to stay soggy. French lavender is undamaged by occasional freezing temperatures, but in areas with sustained hard freezes it should be protected over the winter. Water as needed, but don't let the soil stay soggy. Fertilize in spring and cut back in fall.

Mediterranean Flavors

Although rosemary, sage, oregano, and thyme are different from one another in taste and appearance, they are all woody-stemmed perennials that flourish in the relatively dry Mediterranean climate, which makes them suitable to being grown together in a single container. ¶ Planted together in a striking container, the contrasting appearances of these Mediterranean herbs and their strong resinous scents can make an unusual garden centerpiece. Choose a trailing rosemary and train it to grow downward, covering the edge of your container with its curtain of leaves and blue flowers. Thyme is available in several upright varieties that can be clipped into bush form, along with the sage. Oregano, prone to sprawling, can be clipped asymmetrically, with part of it growing upright and the remainder of its branches arching over the side of the container. ¶ The diverse flavors of rosemary, sage, oregano, and thyme blend into and season all the foods of the Mediterranean—Greek moussaka, Moroccan tangines and stews, Italian breads and pastas, and the grilled meats and vegetables of Spain and Southern France. ¶ **HOW TO DO IT** ¶ Buy a mixture of five or six rosemary, sage, oregano, and thyme plants in 2- or 4-inch pots. Begin with a good-size container, one that is at least 24 inches in diameter and 18 inches deep. Make sure your container has a drainage hole in the bottom. Cover the hole with gravel, small rocks, or bits of broken pottery. ¶ Fill a bucket, bowl, or sink full of water and then submerge the plants, still in their pots, until air bubbles cease to appear. ¶ While the plants are soaking, fill your container with a blend of potting mix and sand. The sand will assist drainage and help to ensure that the plants' roots don't stand in soggy soil. Soak the mixture with water until it is thoroughly moist, then scoop out ✒

Rosemary, Sage, Oregano, and Thyme

Rosmarinus officinalis, Salvia officinalis, Origanum vulgare, Thymus vulgaris

❧

What You Need

5 or 6 plants chosen from varieties named above
Container at least 24 inches in diameter and 18 inches deep
Gravel, small rocks, or bits of broken pottery
Potting mix and sand
Liquid or other fertilizer

❧

Growing Conditions

Three-quarters to a full day of direct sun

❧

When to Buy

In early spring and summer at nurseries and garden centers

❧

When to Plant

Early spring or summer

❧

When to Harvest

Take sprigs after the plants show at least 2 inches of new growth

❧

holes for each of your plants. ¶ Gently remove the plants from their pots, their potting mix intact, and put them into the prepared holes. Fill the holes with potting mix and pat down the surface. Water to fill in any air pockets. ¶ Keep the mix moist, but not soggy, during the first spring and summer of growth. Thereafter, water when the plants show signs of wilt. Above all, do not allow the mix to stay soggy. Fertilize about three weeks after planting and again each spring. ¶ Shape the plant growth as desired. Cut away any dead growth from the sage and oregano in winter, and in climates with hard freezes either apply mulch or overwinter the herbs inside.

Sorrel

orrel is an old-fashioned green, once used primarily as a pot-herb or boiling green and now more commonly used to make more delicate dishes, such as pale green sorrel sauce for salmon and other fish or classic creamy sorrel soup. Sorrel has sword-shaped leaves, and the tiny ones are used whole in salads, where they add a sharp tang. ¶ *The plant has a tendency to spread and may become invasive in the garden. Consequently, gardeners with small spaces hesitate to plant it. However, since sorrel's roots are readily contained in raised wooden planter beds or other containers, we recommend planting this easy-to-grow, flavorful herb.* ¶ **HOW TO DO IT** ¶ Sorrel may be grown from seed or from purchased plants. To grow two or three plants in a pot, choose a container 12 inches across and 12 inches or more deep. Make sure it has a drainage hole in the bottom. Cover the hole with a little gravel, a few small rocks, or bits of broken pottery. ¶ Fill the container with a mixture of one-half potting mix and one-half organic matter such as peat moss. Soak the mixture until it is thoroughly moist. ¶ If you are using seeds, sprinkle them across the surface and press them into the moist mix, covering the seeds with about 1/4 inch of it. If you are using plants, soak them still in their pots in a bucket, bowl, or sinkful of water until air bubbles cease to appear. Scoop out a hole for each plant in the prepared container. Gently remove the plants from their pots, along with their potting mix, and put one plant in each hole. Fill in the holes with the moist mix and pat the surface smooth. Water to fill in any air pockets. ¶ Keep the soil moist, almost soggy, and fertilize every three weeks with a liquid fertilizer during the growth period. If the container becomes overcrowded, thin by dividing or removing some of the plants. Sorrel will die back during the cold winter months, and then put forth new leaves in spring.

Sorrel

Rumex acetosa

❧

What You Need

1 packet seed or 2 or 3 plants, 2- or 4-inch pot size

Container at least 12 inches in diameter and 12 inches deep

Gravel, small rocks, or bits of broken pottery; Potting mix

Organic matter, such as peat moss or well-rotted leaves

Liquid fertilizer

❧

Growing Conditions

A quarter to half-day of direct sun

❧

When to Buy

Seed: in winter and spring from mail-order catalogues; plants: in spring at nurseries or garden centers

❧

When to Plant

Spring or fall in areas without hard freezes

❧

When to Harvest

From seed: take mature leaves in about 90 days, but you can use the thinnings and young leaves earlier; from transplants: take a few leaves after the plants have several inches of new growth

❧

MINT

Mint is very easy to grow once started, and it is almost indestructible. As long as it has abundant water and a little sun, the sturdy mint plant, covered with furred round leaves, grows and multiplies rapidly—too rapidly for some gardens—which makes it a good choice to grow within the confines of a container, or at least a contained space. ¶ Spearmint, peppermint, bergamot, and lemon are a few of the numerous varieties of mint available. Nurseries and garden centers frequently carry three or four different types, and many more may be located through mail-order catalogues. Mint is easily propagated by cuttings, so if you have a friend or neighbor with a thriving plant, ask for a 4- or 5-inch long cutting and put it in a jar of water. In a week or so, when you see the beginnings of roots forming at the nodes along the submerged stem portion, your mint cutting will be ready to plant. ¶ **HOW TO DO IT** ¶ Choose a container about 24 inches in diameter and at least 12 inches deep. Make sure your container has a drainage hole in the bottom. Cover the hole with a little gravel, a few small rocks, or bits of broken pottery. ¶ Fill the container to within 1/2 inch of the rim with potting mix and soak it until it is thoroughly moist, almost soggy. Soak purchased plants, still in their pots, in a sink, bucket, or bowlful of water until air bubbles cease to appear. In the potting mix scoop out holes about 6 inches deep. Gently remove plants from their pots, along with their potting mix, and put them into the holes. Put cuttings rooted in water directly into the holes. Fill in the holes with moist potting mix and pat the surface smooth. Water to fill in any air pockets. ¶ Mint is a water lover and will do best if the potting mix is kept moist at all times. Fertilize every three or four weeks. If the plants start looking leggy and spindly, cut them back to encourage new growth.

Spearmint or Peppermint
Mentha spicata, Mentha peperita

❧

What You Need
5 plants or rooted cuttings
Container 24 inches in diameter and at least 12 inches deep
Gravel, small rocks, or bits of broken pottery
Potting mix
Liquid fertilizer

❧

Growing Conditions
A quarter to a half-day of direct sun

❧

When to Buy
Early spring and summer at nurseries and garden centers and from mail-order catalogues

❧

When to Plant
Spring through summer; also fall in temperate climates

❧

When to Harvest
Start harvesting after there is at least 2 inches of new growth

❧

HERBS TO
GROW IN A
PATCH OF
GROUND

In a patch of ground perhaps only a few feet square, you can plant an herb garden with a few perennial, permanent herbs that will give you pleasure season after season for years to come. You can thus dedicate your garden to the perennials, if you know you love them. You can also mix in two or three annual herbs (those that last only for one season), and reseed those you want again the following year. If you are unwilling to commit to any permanent plantings, you can form a whole herb garden of annuals only. As long as your little garden receives at least a half-day of sun and you water, weed, and tend it with reasonable faithfulness, you can be successful with herbs in this section of any type. ❧ As you choose the herbs for your garden, keep in mind the kind of cooking you do or would like to do, along with the colors and appearance of the herbs you contemplate. Your garden should please you visually when you look at it and tend it, and its harvest should please you in the kitchen. ❧ To our thinking, there is no point taking up the precious space of a small culinary herb garden with an herb you rarely use in the kitchen or with an herb that you personally find unappealing to look at. If you find disorder disconcerting, you may not want the sprawling, occasionally scruffy looking oregano in your garden, for example. If on the other hand the idea of a plant pungent with the scent of the dry hills of Mediterranean islands, where oregano grows wild, seems a splendid thing to have outside your kitchen door, plant it by all means.

ARUGULA IN THE GARDEN

Arugula, also called garden rocket, rocket, and roquette, is a toothsome, nutty-flavored annual that is quickly grown from seed. Young, slightly serrated leaves only three or four weeks old are bright green and quite tender. As the plant matures and grows, often to 2 feet or more, the leaves change to dark green and become more strongly flavored and more markedly serrated. In summer, during the warm weather, arugula goes quickly to seed, and pretty little white blossoms each with a tiny, faint red cross in the center appear. They are peppery but delicate when young and make a good garnish for soups and salads. ¶ To have young leaves over and over again throughout the season, pull up the arugula, roots and all, when you harvest them. Reseed every two or three weeks. An alternative is to cut the leaves when you gather them, leaving the roots to put out new growth, over and over. Using this "cut and come again" method produces new leaves that are similar to mature leaves in taste and texture. ¶ **HOW TO DO IT** ¶ When there is no danger of frost for at least 2 months, scatter the seeds over moist, prepared ground. Cover them with 1/4 inch of soil and pat down. Germination will usually occur within the week. As the seedlings grow, thin to 2 or 3 inches apart. ¶ Keep the garden patch free of weeds. Water the arugula frequently, keeping the soil moist. Reseed every two weeks for successive plantings.

Arugula

Eruca vesicaria subsp. *sativa*

What You Need

1 packet seed

2 to 3 square feet of prepared ground

Growing Conditions

A half- to a full day of direct sun

When to Buy

Year-round from mail-order
seed catalogues

When to Plant

Throughout spring, in late summer,
and through fall; in summer where
the climate is mild

When to Harvest

Young, 3- to 4-inch long leaves are
ready in 20 to 25 days, and full size,
mature leaves in 65 days

FRENCH TARRAGON

French tarragon, also called true tarragon, is grown only from cuttings. Once started it is an explosive herb, sending out shoots in every direction. Two or three plants in a small garden patch will give you tarragon for stuffing chickens by the handful, enough to make a dozen bottles of tarragon vinegar and to flavor sauces all summer long. Having an abundance of tarragon is cause for culinary revelry. ¶ It is easy to grow and to care for. Provide well-worked, rich soil and keep the tarragon watered. When the winter freezes come the tarragon will turn dark reddish-brown, wither, and die back. As the days lengthen in spring and into early summer the tarragon will begin to send up new, grey-green shoots, and your harvest will start all over again. ¶ **HOW TO DO IT** ¶ Buy small, 2-inch pot size tarragon plants—these are rooted cuttings and will quickly take to transplanting. Prior to transplanting them, fill a sink, bucket, or bowl with water and submerge the plants, still in their containers, until air bubbles cease to appear. ¶ In prepared garden soil that is thoroughly moist, dig holes 10 to 12 inches apart and about 6 inches deep for 4-inch pot size plants. If you have larger plants, dig correspondingly larger holes. Gently remove the tarragon plants from their containers, leaving the potting mix intact around the developing roots. ¶ Place the plants, along with the potting mix, into the prepared holes. Fill the holes with soil, packing it gently around the roots. Water to fill in any air pockets. ¶ Keep the soil moist and the garden plot free of weeds. When the plant turns brown and dies back in the winter, cut away all the dead growth, preparing for spring's fresh growth. In extreme cold climates protection may be necessary over the winter. Fertilize as soon as new growth appears in spring.

Tarragon
Artemisia dracunculus

What You Need
1 plant, 4-inch pot size
1 square foot of
prepared ground per plant
Fertilizer

Growing Conditions
At least a half-day of direct sun;
preferably a full day

When to Buy
Spring and summer at nurseries
and garden centers

When to Plant
Spring, when danger of frost has past,
through early summer

When to Harvest
Clip sprigs after the plant has at least
2 inches of new growth

THYME

Thyme is one of the most versatile of all culinary herbs, so if you plant only a single herb variety in your patch of ground, choose common thyme. Five or six plants grown in a small three square-foot area will give you the luxury of using mounds of this clean, woodsy herb to tuck under chicken breasts before broiling them or to layer between chops in a marinade without the slightest worry that you are depleting your garden patch. ¶ *Thyme adapts well to different growing conditions. A shrubby, woody plant when grown in dry conditions, thyme will grow even in rocky soil, once it is well established. On the other hand, well-watered plants overcome their woodiness and become supple, almost lush with densely spaced leaves, barely resembling the same plant grown in relatively dry conditions.* ¶ *There are many varieties of thyme, including some with exotic flavors such as caraway and orange. Some varieties have upright growth habits and others grow in spreading, prostrate forms. For all-around culinary satisfaction, however, in all growing conditions, we recommend common thyme.* ¶ **HOW TO DO IT** ¶ Buy five or six thyme plants in 2- or 4-inch pots. In prepared garden soil that is thoroughly moist, dig holes 8 to 10 inches apart and about 6 inches deep for plants this size. Prior to transplanting, fill a sink, bucket, or bowl with water and submerge the thyme, still in their pots, until bubbles cease to appear. ¶ Gently remove the thyme plants from their containers, leaving the potting mix intact around their roots. Place each plant and its mix in a prepared hole. Fill the holes with soil, packing it gently around the roots. Pat the surface smooth and water to fill in any air pockets. ¶ Water frequently, keeping the soil moist until the plants show several inches of new growth. Keep the garden site free of weeds. In areas with hard winter freezes, mulch the plants around their bases. Fertilize in spring when the first new leaves appear.

OREGANO

A tablespoon of chopped fresh oregano on top of a pizza—any kind of pizza—makes this herb worth its garden space. It is a rambling plant, prone to ungainliness, and grows in every which way. In winter it turns black, and you cannot help but be convinced that it is dead. However, come spring, cut back the shriveled branches and the plant will soon send out long shoots covered with soft green leaves. The more you cut the shoots, the bushier the plants will become with new growth. ¶ Oregano and sweet marjoram are so closely related, it is difficult to tell them apart. Generally speaking oregano has a stronger flavor, larger leaves, and a wilder growth habit. Should you choose sweet marjoram inadvertently, it is not a culinary disaster. Use sweet marjoram just as you would oregano but in larger quantities, to add to pizzas, omelettes, and salad dressings and to make Italian, Greek, and other Mediterranean foods. ¶ **HOW TO DO IT** ¶ Buy a 2-or 4-inch pot size oregano plant. One plant will provide plenty of seasoning for most kitchens. Prior to transplanting it, fill a sink, bucket, or bowl with water and submerge the oregano, still in its container, until bubbles cease to appear. ¶ In prepared garden soil that is thoroughly moist, dig a hole 10 inches wide and 6 inches deep. Gently remove the oregano plant and its potting mix from its container and place the plant and the mix in the prepared hole. Fill the hole with soil, packing it gently around the roots. Pat down the surface and water to fill in any air pockets. ¶ Keep cutting shoots as desired for use or, if you wish, cut all the shoots back for a tidy appearance. New ones will follow. Water only when thoroughly dry. Keep the garden site free of weeds. Mulch around the base of the plant in areas with harsh winters. In spring, after all danger of frost has past, prune back the dead branches to within 4 or 5 inches of the base of the plant and fertilize.

Oregano
Origanum vulgare

What You Need
1 oregano plant, 2- to 4-inch pot size
2 square feet prepared ground
Fertilizer

Growing Conditions
A least a half-day of direct sun

When to Buy
Spring or early summer at nurseries or garden centers

When to Plant
In spring, after any danger of frost, through midsummer

When to Harvest
Once the plant has put forth about 4 inches of new growth, start to harvest the leaves

LARGE-LEAF ITALIAN BASIL

Easily grown from seed or from transplants, large-leaf Italian basil is the quintessential summer herb. The flavors of summer's vegetables—tomatoes, squash, eggplants, beans—are heightened and intensified when liberally seasoned with basil, one of the most fragrant of all herbs. A few basil leaves clipped from the garden and brought into the kitchen will quickly fill the room with their aroma. ¶ Large-leaf Italian basil is extremely productive, growing up to 2 feet tall, and six or seven plants will provide the ordinary kitchen with a plethora of basil leaves. Even though the plants will send up long, flowering seed stalks in late summer, initiating the end of their vegetative period of growth, if you cut back the stalks when they appear and keep the plants well watered, bushy leaf growth will continue until the plants are finally killed by the first hard frosts. ¶ **HOW TO DO IT** ¶ Plant basil seeds 1 inch apart and 1/4 inch deep in moist, prepared garden ground. Pat the surface smooth. Keep the soil moist until germination occurs and the seedlings have several leaves. Thin seedlings to 8 inches apart. ¶ If you are planting basil transplants, fill a bowl, bucket, or sink with water and soak the transplants, still in their pots, until air bubbles cease to appear. ¶ Dig holes 6 inches deep and 8 inches apart in moist, prepared garden soil. Gently remove the plants and their potting mix from their pots and put one plant in each hole. Fill the hole in with moist soil, and pat the surface smooth. Water to fill in any air pockets. ¶ Fertilize after three to four weeks of growth. Keep the soil moist but not soggy. Basil will become hot and bitter if grown in dry conditions. Cut off flowering seed stalks to encourage bushy leaf growth.

Large-Leaf Italian Basil
Ocimum basilicum

❧

What You Need
*1 packet seed or 6 or 7 seedlings,
2- or 4-inch pot size
2 to 3 square feet of prepared ground
Fertilizer*

❧

Growing Conditions
Three-quarters to a full day of direct sun

❧

When to Buy
*Seed: in early spring or summer
Seedlings: in late spring and
early summer*

❧

When to Plant
*Late spring or early summer when
the ground has warmed*

❧

When to Harvest
*From seed: wait 75 days, but
take a few leaves after the plants are 6
to 8 inches tall, in about 55 days
From transplants: take leaves after the
plants have 2 inches or more
of new growth*

❧

HERBS FOR

A SENSE

OF VAST

VISTAS

*S*ome herbs have an ability to create a visual sense of vastness and abundance while growing in a small space. In some instances, nasturtiums and violets, for example, the leaf shape and growth pattern cause this sense of expansiveness. ❧ A handful of nasturtium seeds can produce vines that will blanket a wall and overgrow a walkway. A dozen violet plants will reseed themselves during their first season, and by their second season they will have made a solid patch of heart-shaped, glossy green leaves with hundreds of deep-purple flowers. Probably no massed planting, however, is as dramatic as English lavender in full bloom. Bristled like porcupines, the round, bushy mounds of the grey-green plant are covered with dozens and dozens of 18-inch long stems, their tips covered with tiny, honey-sweet blossoms. ❧ When grown in open fields, massed rows of lavender plants reach out to one another to cover the soil with a hovering, incandescent purple hue. Even four or five English lavender plants grown together in a clump create the luxuriant and glowing sensation of a much larger planting. ❧ Variegated sage varieties with purple, red, gold, white, and green leaves all planted together make a good choice for filling areas with little water. Two or three plants edging a staircase or garden corner are enough to create a muted block of subtle colors. ❧ To plant for maximum drama, whether with lavender, sage, violets, or nasturtiums, keep the plants close together. Initially it may seem demoralizing to see the intermittent small plants with great gaps of ground between them. It may even appear to you impossible that such tiny plants will grow so large that they will touch, overlap, and entwine with their neighbors. In the case of nasturtiums and sage, this miracle will occur within the year. Lavender, however, will require up to three years before it acquires its full size. ❧ Have patience and you will be rewarded with a blanket of pattern and color, even in a small space.

VIOLETS

Although generally grown from divisions or runners, violets produce and drop a great quantity of seed, which makes them quick to naturalize. Even a few square feet of violets, planted in rich, moist soil, will soon produce a carpet of green and purple. If you locate the violets near a stone wall or path, beneath the edge of a spreading tree, or among tangled ivy, they will soon naturalize there and create a sense of the forest or meadows where they grow wild. ¶ In the nineteenth century, candied violet flowers were a popular sweet. Sometimes they were served alone as a confection, and other times the crystalline flowers were used to decorate pastries and cakes. Translucent jellies of royal purple were also made of violets and served at tea time. ¶ In today's adventuresome restaurants, fresh violets are tossed into mixed green salads, or used by the handful to flavor a creamy vanilla custard with the flowers' perfume. ¶ As with all edible flowers, be absolutely certain that they have not been sprayed or otherwise treated with a potentially harmful spray. ¶ **HOW TO DO IT** ¶ Violet plants are generally sold in half-gallon pots. Fill a large basin, sink, or tub full of water and submerge the plants, still in their pots, until air bubbles cease to appear. ¶ In prepared, thoroughly moist garden soil, dig holes one and a half times as deep and as wide as the violet pots. Space the holes about 10 inches apart. Gently remove the violet plants from their pots, along with their potting mix, and put one in each prepared hole. Fill the hole with moist soil and pat the surface firmly around the roots. Water to fill any air pockets. ¶ Keep the soil moist, especially during blooming season. The plants will begin to die back during the hot summer months and will go dormant during winter. Cover in winter with a layer of dead leaves or branches. Fertilize in spring after the first new leaves have appeared. After several years, dig them up and divide and replant them.

Violet
Viola odorata

❧

What You Need
10 to 12 violets plants, usually sold in half-gallon pots
10 to 12 square feet of prepared ground
Fertilizer

❧

Growing Conditions
A quarter to a half-day of direct sun

❧

When to Buy
Fall through summer

❧

When to Plant
Early spring and summer

❧

When to Harvest
Take violets as soon as blooms appear

❧

MASSED LAVENDER

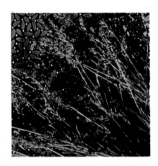

Fully mature, English lavender plants in full bloom present fragrant 3-foot hemispheres that have few parallels for scent or beauty. To create a sense of mass, plant them three or four to a grouping. During late summer, fall, and winter the leaves of your lavender plants will make a wall of soft grey color and texture. The hues of the plants will subtly change as the new, light green growth appears in early spring, followed by budding flower spikes. By midsummer the plants' color will have changed to a vibrant purple. ¶ In Southern France, "boules" of lavender are common swimming pool borders and are planted to make colorful walls between flagstone patios and grass lawns. In other planting styles, two or three lavender plants are grouped around mailboxes, at the edges of driveways, and near doorways. ¶ English lavender is easily grown and requires minimum effort on the part of the gardener. Like other lavenders, it may be used to flavor creams and other sweet dishes and also used in combination with other herbs, such as mint, to make infusions. Tea merchants sometimes sell a traditional mix of Earl Grey tea blended with lavender blossom. The lavender gives its delicious aroma and a hauntingly exotic finish to the taste of the tea. ¶ **HOW TO DO IT** ¶ English lavender is generally grown from cuttings. These are usually sold in six-packs or 2-inch pots. The small cuttings will grow a foot or more and bloom within their first year of growth. One-year-old plants may be purchased as well, generally in a 1-gallon-size container. Plan on three or four lavender plants for a 12-square foot area. ¶ Fill a large bucket, sink, or bowl with water and submerge the lavender plants, still in their packs or pots, until air bubbles cease to appear. ¶ In thoroughly moist, prepared garden soil, dig holes 6 inches ✔

English Lavender
Lavendula angustifolia

❧

What You Need
4 or 5 plants, 2-inch pot size preferred
10 to 12 square feet of prepared ground
Fertilizer

❧

Growing Conditions
At least a half-day of direct sun

❧

When to Buy
In spring from nurseries, garden centers,
and mail-order catalogues

❧

When to Plant
Spring and summer

❧

When to Harvest
When plants produce bloom; they
may bloom several months after planting
or the following summer season

❧

deep and 3 feet apart for each 2-inch size pot. Gently pull the plants and their potting mix from their packs or pots. Put one plant in each hole, packing soil around the roots. Pat the surface smooth and water to fill in any air pockets. Keep soil moist but not soggy during spring and summer. In fall or winter, when growth has stopped, clip and discard old stems. Fertilize within one week of planting and each spring after the first tips of new growth appear.

VINING NASTURTIUMS

Claude Monet, the famous French Impressionist painter, planted acres of gardens at his home in Giverny, France. He was fascinated by the interplay of light with the changing shapes and colors of the flowers, and spent the last thirty years of his life recording the interplay on canvas throughout the seasons. ¶ Vining nasturtiums figured large in Monet's garden design and paintings. Masses of vining nasturtiums were planted on both sides of the entire length of the Grande Allée that was the heart of the garden. The nasturtiums' allure changed with each season, because their growth constantly redefined the space of the walkway. ¶ In spring the round green nasturtium leaves and first buds appeared in a trim, orderly fashion at the edge of the walkway. By summertime the vines were a foot or more high and several times as wide, their twisting mass creeping toward the middle of the walk and twining upward along the walls of the raised beds filled with dahlias and other summer bulbs. By the time autumn arrived the nasturtiums had spread in voluminous mass across the 30-foot wide allée, until only the few feet down the middle of the walk remained uncovered. ¶ The same effect can be achieved anywhere you have a walkway, even a small one, edged by a foot or two of open ground. A brick path, cobbled stepping-stones, or an asphalt driveway will all succumb to nasturtiums. ¶ The long, shapely vines, loaded with leaves and blossoms, make striking cut flower arrangements too. Several clipped vines each 2 feet or longer and held in a simple glass or vase make a striking and graceful arrangement. ¶ For culinary use, the peppery leaves and sweet flowers are delicious added to salads. The flowers, crushed with butter, salt, and pepper, make a flavorful spread for fish and steaks. ¶ **HOW TO DO IT** ¶ To fill a 10 foot by 1 foot space along a walkway, you will need 120 to 150 seeds of vining nasturtiums, or about 1 ounce. Bush-type varieties will not produce long vines. Soak the seeds overnight in warm water. This allows the seed to fill itself with water and to start ✐

Nasturtium, Vining Type
Tropaeolum majus
❧

What You Need
About 1 ounce or 120 to 150 seeds
10 square feet of prepared ground
Fertilizer
❧

Growing Conditions
One-half to three-quarters of a day
of direct sun
❧

When to Buy
Winter and spring from mail-order
catalogues; spring and summer at
garden centers and nurseries
❧

When to Plant
In spring when there is no longer any
danger of hard frost; also in fall in
temperate climates
❧

When to Harvest
Pick the first leaves and early blooms
in about 75 days
❧

the germination process before being planted. ¶ Plant the seeds 1/2 inch deep and about 4 inches apart in thoroughly moist, prepared soil in a location that receives at least a half-day of sun. Keep the soil moist until germination occurs and adequately watered thereafter. Nasturtiums flourish in wet soil and cool damp weather. ¶ Fertilize every 5 or 6 weeks for lush growth. Nasturtiums will reseed themselves in moderate climates but must be replanted each year in areas with freezing temperatures, as they are killed by frosts.

Shades of sage

H ues of red, purple, gold, green, and cream are all evident in the leaf colors of the different varieties of sage. When planted together en masse, these sage plants make a soft palette of muted color. In bloom, the plants send up long spikes tipped with purple blossoms that attract butterflies, bees, and hummingbirds. ¶ Since sage needs relatively little water once it is started, it can provide color, pattern, and texture in your landscape where water-loving plants cannot succeed. ¶ Start with small pots of different colored sages. Once planted and nurtured in spring, the plants will quickly grow to a foot or more before winter's cold arrives. In areas with hard freezes, however, the plants require mulching or other protection. ¶ For the most impressive effect, mass a dozen or more plants. Choose a single variety, red and green variegated, for example, if you want a monochromatic mass of color, or a mix of different varieties for a dappled effect. Sage is particularly useful on hillsides and sloping banks where watering may be difficult, but don't hesitate to use it to border a bulb garden or front walkway. ¶ Multicolored sage can be used in cooking just as you would common sage. The leaves, with their red, purple, and creamy golden hues, make fanciful garnishes for grilled meats and roasts. ¶ **HOW TO DO IT** ¶ Although sage may be grown from seed, germination may be erratic. For more certain success, we recommend starting with plants in a 4-inch pot size. ¶ Fill a sink, bucket, or large bowl with water. Submerge the plants, still in their containers, and let soak until air bubbles cease to appear. ¶ In prepared moist soil—thoroughly watered—scoop out holes large enough to hold the sage plants. Place the holes about 10 inches apart. Gently remove the plants and their ✐

Golden Sage, Purple Sage, Tricolor Sage

Salvia officinalis: 'Icterina', 'Purpurascens', 'Tricolor'

❧

What You Need

10 to 12 variegated sage plants chosen from varieties listed above, 4-inch pot size

10 to 12 square feet of prepared ground

Fertilizer

❧

Growing Conditions

Three-quarters to a full day of direct sun

❧

When to Buy

Early spring from nurseries and garden centers

❧

When to Plant

Early spring when there is no danger of frost

❧

When to Harvest

Take leaves after the plant shows at least 2 inches of new growth

❧

potting mix from the containers. Put one plant in each hole and fill the hole with soil. Pat down the surface and water to fill in any air pockets. ¶ Water the plants again when a knife or trowel inserted 2 inches deep shows dry ground, or when the plants begin to look limp. Do not overwater. Keep the ground free of weeds and cultivate several times a year. Fertilize in early spring just as new growth begins to appear.

F R E S H
HERBS IN
THE KITCHEN
PANTRY

The ultimate joy of growing fresh herbs is using them in cooking. Throughout the book we have included suggestions for using specific herbs, and in this chapter we are providing several basic recipes—one for herbal oil, one for herbal vinegar, a sorbet recipe and one for a granita, and a biscotti recipe. ❧ Oils infused with the essence of different herbs are quite simple to make and to store. Their uses are varied and healthful, as they can have some of the complexity and depth of flavor that butter- and cream-based sauces acquire but without the rich butterfat. ❧ Like oils, infused vinegars are simple to make and to store. There is perpetual delight in discovering the subtly different tastes that can be achieved by adding different herbs in varying quantities to various vinegars and then experimenting with their use. For example, basil vinegar is an obvious choice for tomatoes, but it can also be used to deglaze a pan of sautéed chicken breasts. ❧ Sorbets are one of the least complex yet most elegant and refreshing of frozen desserts. Although fruit sorbets are very much in fashion because of their taste and their low fat and calorie content, herb sorbets are not as common. In the past herb sorbets were served not as sweets at the end of the meal but as "palate refreshers" between courses of a multicoursed meal. Today herbs in sorbets are likely to be combined with fruits, or used on their own with a sweetener added. ❧ The light perfumes of rose-scented geranium, lavender, and lemon thyme give a hint of mysterious flavoring to Italian biscotti. These crunchy, twice-cooked cookies use relatively little sugar, instead relying for flavoring on nuts, flavor essences, herbs, and spices. ❧ As you grow and use fresh herbs, you will discover as we have that they can be used every day.

Herb-infused oils

Olive oil, walnut oil, sunflower oil, or any other good-quality vegetable oil can be flavored with fresh herbs, but remember that herbs will not turn a poor-quality, inferior product into something special. The herbs you are going to use should be picked in the morning as soon as they are free of morning dew or moisture. ¶ Although the quantities of herbs needed to fully flavor an oil can vary somewhat, a general rule is to fill the container one-third full with fresh crushed herbs, then fill to the top with the oil. Remove the herbs when the oil is sufficiently flavored and optionally add a sprig of fresh herbs to the finished bottle for decoration. ¶ Since fresh herbs with high water content such as basil and mint discolor and may even mold after several weeks, it is best to omit them from the finished product. On the other hand, the woody herbs are good choices, including fresh bay laurel, lavender, oregano, rosemary, sage, and thyme. **ROSEMARY OLIVE OIL** ¶ Rosemary oil brings a resinous, pungent taste to pizzas when drizzled on top of the fresh pizza dough before the toppings are added. Tomatoes, onions, leeks, or other vegetables can be cooked down to their very essence in rosemary oil, and then seasoned with a little fresh thyme to make a confit to accompany pork chops or roast beef, for example. Rosemary oil also makes a superb marinating oil for meats and vegetables. **HOW TO DO IT** ¶ Crush the rosemary slightly and put it in the jar. Cover the rosemary with the olive oil and cover the jar with a lid or with wax paper well secured with string or a rubber band. Put the covered jar inside in a sunny window or outside in a sunny location. Let the jar stand for about 10 days. Taste the oil occasionally by pouring a little on a piece of bread. ¶ When you find the oil is sufficiently flavored, remove the rosemary and discard it or use it in cooking, as it will be fully saturated with olive oil. ¶ Put the rosemary oil into pretty glass bottles or jars, and if desired, add a sprig of fresh rosemary. Seal with a cork or lid and store in a cool, dark place. It will keep several months. ¶ Makes approximately 32 ounces.

Rosemary Olive Oil

❧

What You Need
3 cups fresh rosemary, cut into
1-inch lengths
A large, clean, dry glass jar with a
large mouth and a lid
32 ounces fruity olive oil
Smaller bottles with corks or
screw-top lids

❧

HERB-INFUSED VINEGARS

onderful, well-flavored herbal vinegars can be made using the good-quality, relatively inexpensive cider and red and white wine vinegars that are readily available. White wine vinegar infused with French tarragon is a classic herb vinegar, but only one of many possibilities. In general, herbs that have a slightly sharp or acidic taste make good flavoring for vinegars. Any of the basils, calendula, cilantro, lemon thyme, and mint are good examples. ¶ Herb flower blossoms make delicately flavored, jewel-toned vinegars that are especially complimentary with fruits and useful in deglazing. Violets, lavender blossoms, and sage blossoms all are suitable for these lighter vinegars. ¶ **VIOLET-BLOSSOM VINEGAR** ¶ Violet-blossom vinegar is a light garnet shade with a faintly perfumed taste. It can be sprinkled over a salad of tender spring greens (perhaps with fresh violets tossed in the salad as well) or added to the poaching liquid of a salmon filet or other delicate-fleshed fish. ¶ **HOW TO DO IT** ¶ Put the blossoms in the clean jar, cover with the vinegar, and seal with the lid. Keep the jar in a sunny windowsill or sunny location outside for about ten days, until the vinegar has absorbed the essence of the violets. ¶ Strain the flavored vinegar, using a funnel lined with a coffee filter or cheesecloth. Add a few fresh violet petals. ¶ Makes about 16 ounces.

Violet-Blossom Vinegar

≋

What You Need

1 cup violet blossoms, slightly
crushed, stems removed
Clean 16-ounce glass jar with a large
mouth and lid
16 ounces white wine vinegar

≋

HERB SORBETS

Sorbets are icy, refreshing mixtures of frozen sugar, water, and flavorings. To the usual flavorings—fruit purées, fruit juices, wine, coffee, tea, or liqueurs—herbs or herb essences may be added, or herbs may also serve as the primary flavoring. ¶ Herbal sorbets can be made as "palate refreshers" by using a reduced amount of sugar (as in the second recipe below), a style in which the flavor of the herb predominates. Good choices for palette refreshers are mint, rosemary, lemon thyme, and lemon verbena. ¶ Dessert sorbets made with herbs often include fruit as well. Acidic fruits such as limes, oranges, and kumquats add fruit flavor and some sweetness without overpowering the taste of the herbs. ¶ Sorbets are made using ice cream freezers and may also be made in ice cube trays and then frozen in the freezer. In the ice cube tray method, the sorbet is frozen until it is semisolid, then it is taken out of the tray, put in a bowl, and whipped with an electric beater or in a blender or food processor until the sorbet is in bits the size of popcorn kernels. Then it is returned to the ice cube tray and frozen again until it is solid. Both methods are effective. ¶ **DOUBLE LEMON DESSERT SORBET** ¶ *This simple and refreshing sorbet plays upon the dual tastes of tart lemon juice and zesty lemon thyme, sweetened with sugar. Serve with a crunchy sugar cookie.* ¶ **HOW TO DO IT** ¶ Heat the water to boiling in a small saucepan and add the thyme. Reduce heat and simmer for 5 minutes. Remove from heat, cover, and set aside to steep overnight. ¶ The next day, strain the herb-infused water. In a medium saucepan, heat the infused water with the sugar and bring to a rolling boil. Remove from heat and let cool to room temperature, then add the lemon juice. Freeze in an ice cream freezer, following the manufacturer's directions, or in ice cube trays. ¶ To serve, garnish with sprigs of fresh lemon thyme. ¶ Makes about 1 quart. ¶ **MINT PALATE REFRESHER** ¶ *Serve this delicately mint flavored granita—a grainier, less smooth version of* ✒

Double Lemon Dessert Sorbet

❧

What You Need

1 1/4 cups water

3 tablespoons lemon thyme leaves, crushed

2 1/2 cups sugar

1 1/2 cups lemon juice

❧

Mint Palate Refresher

❧

What You Need

1 1/2 cups water

1 cup fresh mint leaves, crushed

3/4 cup sugar

1 1/2 cups white wine, such as

Chablis or Reisling

❧

sorbet—after a hearty meat dish, followed by a selection of cheeses, for example, or after a rich fish soup and before a roast leg of lamb. To sweeten this dish for a dessert, it can be accompanied by minted chocolates. ¶ **HOW TO DO IT** ¶ In a small saucepan, bring the water to a boil and add the mint leaves. Reduce the heat and simmer for 5 minutes. Remove from the heat, cover, and let steep overnight. ¶ The next day, strain the infused water and put it in a medium-sized saucepan along with the sugar. Bring it to a rolling boil. Let cool, then add the wine and freeze in an ice cream maker or ice cube trays. It will be grainier and not frozen as solidly as sorbet. ¶ Serve the granita slightly thawed, garnished with fresh mint. ¶ Makes about 1 quart.

HERB-FLAVORED BISCOTTI

Biscotti can be made using any number of different herbs, nuts, spices, and seeds. They can be dipped in chocolate or iced with flavored frosting to achieve greater sweetness. Because they keep well without losing their flavor or texture, they are a good choice to make ahead and to keep on hand in tins. ¶ Try adding a tablespoon of finely chopped rose-scented geranium leaves or lemon thyme to almond biscotti, for example, or a tablespoon of chopped mint leaves to biscotti destined to be chocolate dipped. Be sure to mince the herbs or blossoms to a minuscule size so that they appear only as tiny flecks in the finished cookies. ¶ Biscotti are wonderful dipping cookies, because without crumbling they absorb the coffee, tea, chocolate, wine, or liqueur into which they are dipped. Their crunchy texture goes well with the smoothness of ice cream or sorbets, too. ¶ **LAVENDER-BLOSSOM BISCOTTI** ¶ The unexpected hint of lavender perfume makes a good complement to double vanilla ice cream or a sweet dessert wine, such as marsala or a late-harvest Reisling. ¶ This recipe is from The Italian Baker, by Carol Field (Harper & Row, 1985). The original recipe calls for anise, but here lavender blossoms are used instead.

¶ **HOW TO DO IT** ¶ Preheat an oven to 375 degrees. ¶ Beat the eggs and sugar in a mixer bowl until the mixture forms a slowly dissolving ribbon when the beaters are lifted, 5 to 10 minutes. Mix in the vanilla and lemon zest. Sift the flour and salt. Directly over the egg mixture, sift again with the baking powder. Fold gently into the egg mixture. Stir in the lavender blossoms. ¶ Spoon the batter into a pastry bag fitted with a plain tip. Pipe the batter in strips, 4 inches long and 1 inch wide, onto buttered baking sheets. The piped batter should look like large ladyfingers. ¶ Bake at 375° until slightly crisp and brown around the edges, about 20 minutes. Remove from the oven. Reduce the heat to 325 degrees. Cut each strip in half on the diagonal and bake on the baking sheet 5 to 10 minutes longer. Cool on racks. ¶ Makes 24 biscotti.

Lavender-Blossom Biscotti

❦

What You Need

4 eggs, at room temperature

3/4 cup sugar

1 teaspoon vanilla extract

Grated zest of 1/2 lemon

1 1/2 cups all-purpose flour

1/4 teaspoon salt

1/4 teaspoon baking powder

2 teaspoons finely minced fresh lavender blossoms

❦

Information and Sources

Some companies charge for their catalogs. Call first to check.

W. Atlee Burpee & Co.
P.O. Box 5114
Warminster, PA 18974
(215) 674-9633
Seeds only. Burpee offers an all-purpose catalogue with a standard selection of seeds.

Herb Society of America, Inc.
9019 Kirtland Chardon
Mentor, OH 44060
(216) 256-0514

Heirloom Garden Seeds
P.O. Box 138
Guerneville, CA 95446
(707) 869-0967
Seeds only. This catalogue features old-time, nonhybrid seeds, and it offers ten different varieties of basil.

Nichols Garden Nursery
1190 North Pacific Highway
Albany, OR 97321
(503) 928-9280
Seeds and plants. Plants are shipped only in spring and fall.

Redwood City Seed Company
P.O. Box 361
Redwood City, CA 94064
(415) 325-7333
Seeds only. The company carries seeds but features unusual varieties from all over the world. Look for three kinds of cilantro.

Shepherd's Garden Seeds
6119 Highway 9
Felton, CA 95018
(408) 335-5216
(408) 333-2080 Fax
(203) 496-1418 Fax
Seeds and plants. A limited selection of herbs, an edible flower collection, and a selection of small plants are available by mail.

The Cook's Garden
P.O. Box 535
Londonberry, VT 05148
(802) 824-3400
(802) 824-3027 Fax
Seeds only. Cook's carries nine types of basil plus many annual and perennial herbs.

BIBLIOGRAPHY

Richters Herbs
Goodwood, Ontario
L0C 1A0
Canada
(416) 640-6677
(416) 640-6641 Fax
Seeds and plants. Richters will ship plants internationally but only when there is no local frost, roughly April to October. Extensive selection and excellent information.

Foxhill Farm
443 West Michigan Avenue
P.O. Box 9
Parma, MI 49269
(517) 531-3179
(517) 531-3179 Fax
Plants, year-round. Foxhill Farms carries a comprehensive selection of scented geraniums and topiaries of lavender, rosemary, rose geranium, myrtle, and sweet bay. Also espaliers of lavender. Many varieties of basil and rosemary.

Taylors Herb Gardens
1535 Lone Oak Road
Vista, CA 92084
(619) 727-3485
(619) 727-0289 Fax
Seeds and plants. Taylors ships plants all year long from an extensive selection, and offers excellent information. Reserve your catalogue for February mailing in a request by the previous December.

Culpepper, Nicholas.
Complete Herbal.
Reprint of 1826 edition:
Harvey Sales, 1981.

Hartmann, Hudson T., et al.
Plant Propagation Principles and Practices.
Fifth edition. New Jersey:
Prentice-Hall, 1990.

Holt, Geraldene.
Geraldene Holt's Complete Book of Herbs.
New York: Henry Holt, 1992.

Hortus Third Dictionary.
New York: Macmillan, 1976.

Larkcom, Joy.
Vegetables from Small Gardens.
Second edition. London:
Faber and Faber Limited, 1986.

Muenscher, Walter Conrad, and
Rice, Myron Arthur.
Garden Spice & Wild Pot-Herbs.
Ithaca, New York:
Cornell University Press, 1955.

Zabar, Abbie.
The Potted Herb.
New York:
Stewart, Tabori & Chang, Inc., 1988.

INDEX

Acknowledgments

A very special thank you to Bill LeBlond and Caroline Herter, our editors at Chronicle Books, and Michael Carabetta, Chronicle Book's art director, for their unflinching enthusiasm and guidance as this book and its companion, *Beautiful Bulbs* evolved. ¶ We also wish to thank Leslie Jonath at Chronicle Books for being there at all times when needed. ¶ Thank you to Carey Charlesworth, our editor, for her time and patience on the project. ¶ Our enduring thanks to Jim Schrupp and Warren Roberts for the time and technical expertise they contributed to this book and to *Beautiful Bulbs*. ¶ Thank you, Alta Tingle, Lynn Tingle, and the entire staff of *The Gardener* in Berkeley, California, for your generous contributions of ideas, time, and lovely wares (see pages 26, 79, 84). ¶ A special thanks to Stuart Dixon and all the staff of Stonefree Farms in Davis and Watsonville, California, for always saying yes, no matter how strange the request seemed. ¶ Thank you to the East Bay Nursery, Berkeley, California, and to Whiting Nursery, St. Helena, California, for allowing us to borrow plants and accessories. ¶ We were very fortunate to work with two wonderful stylists, Dorothy Coil, who specializes in gardens, and Michaele Thunen, who is as adept and resourceful with herbs as she is with flowers. Thank you both. ¶ Finally, we wish to thank our families and friends, especially Bruce LeFaveur, who throughout the years, have shared with us their love of herbs and all manner of growing things. ¶ An enthusiastic congratulations to Aufuldish & Warinner for giving our vision a beautiful reality.

We wish to thank all the generous and gracious people who opened their homes and gardens to us for photography.

❧

Dr. Jay Vance,
of Berkeley, California;
The Boonville Hotel
(see pages 62, 73);
Apple Farm,
Philo, California;
French Laundry Restaurant,
St. Helena, California
(see pages 6, 34, 45, 56, 74);
Susan Mills and family,
of Berkeley, California;
Anne Cutting,
of St. Helena, California;
Kathleen Stewart,
of St. Helena, California;
Beringer Winery,
St. Helena, California
(see pages 10, 12, 17, 18, 53, 60);
Carolee Luper,
of St. Helena, California;
Susan Kenward,
of St. Helena, California.

❧